TRADITIONAL FOLKSONGS & BALLADS OF
SCOTLAND

40 COMPLETE SONGS, COLLECTED, ARRANGED AND EDITED BY
John Loesberg

Volume Two

Ossian
Cork
Glasgow
Loughborough
New Hampshire

OSSIAN PUBLICATIONS LTD., IRELAND
(Publishing Dept.)
P.O. Box 84, Cork

OSSIAN PUBLICATIONS SCOTLAND
9 Rosebery Crescent
Edinburgh EH12 5JP

OSSIAN PUBLICATIONS U.K.
Unit 3, Prince William Rd.
Loughborough

OSSIAN PUBLICATIONS USA
RR8 Box 374
Loudon, New Hampshire
03301

OMB 94
ISBN 0 946005 79 6

'Without music, life would be a mistake'

F.W. Nietsche

I Aince Lo'ed a Lass

♩ = 108

When I saw my love tae the kirk go
Wi' bride and bride maidens she made a fine show
And I followed on wi' a hairt fu' o' woe
For she's gone tae be wed tae anither.

When I saw my love sit doon tae dine
I sat doon beside her and poured oot the wine
And I drank tae the lassie that should hae been mine,
But she's gone tae be wed tae anither.

The men o' yon forest they askit o' me
'How many strawberries grow in the saut sea ?'
I answered them back wi' a tear in my e'e
'How many ships sail in the forest ?'

O dig me a grave and dig it sae deep
And cover it owre wi' flooers sae sweet
And I will lie doon there and tak' a lang sleep,
And maybe in time I'll forget her.

OMB 94

The Road to the Isles

♩ = 88

A ... **D** ... **(F#m)**

1 A far croo - nin' is pul - lin' me a - way, As

D ... **A** ... **E**

4 take I wi' my cro - mak to the road. The

A ... **D**

6 far Cool - ins are put - tin' love on me, As

A ... **E** ... **A** ... Chorus:

8 step I wi' the sun - light for my load. Sure, by

D ... **(F#m)**

11 Tum - mel and Loch Ran - noch and Loch - a - ber I will go, By

D ... **A** ... **E**

13 hea - ther tracks wi' hea - ven in their wiles; If it's

A ... **(F#m)**

15 think - in' in your in - ner heart brag - gart's in my step, You've

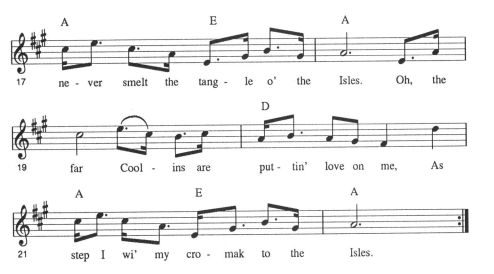

17 ne - ver smelt the tang - le o' the Isles. Oh, the

19 far Cool - ins are put - tin' love on me, As

21 step I wi' my cro - mak to the Isles.

It's by 'Sheil water the track is to the west,
By Aillort and by Morar to the sea,
The cool cresses I am thinkin' o' for pluck,
And bracken for a wink on Mother knee.

It's the blue Islands are pullin' me away,
Their laughter puts the leap upon the lame,
The blue Islands from the Skerries to the Lews,
Wi' heather honey taste upon each name.

OMB 94

Scotland the Brave

♩ = 152

C

1 Hark, when the night is fal - ling; Hear! hear the pipes are cal - ling

F   C   G

5 Loud - ly and proud - ly cal - ling, down thro' the glen.

C

9 There where the hills are slee - ping, now feel the blood a- leap-ing,

F   C   G   C

13 high, as the spir - its of the old High - land men.

Chorus G   C

17 Tower - ing in gal - lant fame, Scot - land my moun - tain hame,

Am   G   F   G

21 High may your proud stan - dards glo - ri - ous - ly wave.

C

25 Land of my high en - deav - our, land of the shin - ing sil - ver,

Land of my heart for - ev - er, Scot - land the brave.

High in the misty Highlands,
Out by the purple islands,
Brave are the hearts that beat beneath Scottish Skies.
Wild are the winds to meet you,
Staunch are the friends that greet you,
Kind as the love that shines from fair maidens' eyes.

OMB 94

Hey the Dusty Miller

♩ = 108

Hey, the dusty Miller,
And his dusty sack;
Leeze me on the calling
Fills the dusty peck:
Hey, the dusty Miller,
And his dusty sack;
Leeze me on the calling
Fills the dusty peck:
Fills the dusty peck,
Brings the dusty siller;
I wad gie my coatie
For the dusty Miller.

Green Grow the Rashes O

There's nought but care on ev'-ry han,' In ev'-ry hour that pas-ses, O, What sig- ni- fies the life o' man, An 'twere na for the las-sies, O ?

Chorus
Green grow the rash- es, O; Green grow the rash- es, O; The sweet-est hours that e'er I spent, Are spent a- mang the las- ses, O !

2 The war'ly race may riches chase,
  An' riches still may fly them, O;
  An' tho' at last they catch them fast,
  Their hearts can ne'er enjoy them, O.

  Chorus

3 But gie me a cannie hour at e'en,
  My arms about my dearie, O;
  An' war'ly cares, an' war'ly men,
  May a' gae tapsalteerie, O !

  Chorus

4 For you sae douce, ye sneer at this;
  Ye're nought but senseless asses, O:
  The wisest man the warl' e'er saw,
  He dearly lov'd the lasses, O.

  Chorus

5 Auld Nature swears, the lovely dears
  Her noblest work she classes, O:
  Her prentice han' she try'd on man,
  An' then she made the lasses, O.

  Chorus

OMB 94

Johnnie Cope

♩ = 120

When Charlie look'd the letter upon,
He drew his sword the scabbard from;
'Come follow me, my merry men,
An' we'll meet Johnnie Cope in the mornin.'

Chorus

'Now Johnnie be as guid's your word,
Come let us try baith fire an' sword,
An' dinna flee like a frichtet bird,
That's chas'd frae its nest in the mornin.'

Chorus

When Johnnie Cope he hear o' this,
He thocht it wadna be amiss
To hae a horse in readiness
To flee awa in the mornin.'

Chorus

'Fie, Johnnie, noo get up and rin,
The Highland bagpipes mak a din,
It's best to sleep in a hale skin,
For 'twill be a bloody mornin.'

Chorus

When Johnnie Cope to Berwick came,
They spier'd at him 'Where's a' your men ?'
'The deil confound me gin I ken,
For I left them a' in the mornin.'

Chorus

13

Horo, My Nut-Brown Maiden

♩ = 116

Ho- ro, my nut-brown mai- den, Hi- ri, my nut- brown mai- den, Ho-
ro, ro, mai - den. For she's the maid for me. Her
eye so mild - ly bea - ming, Her look so frank and free, In
wak - ing and in dream - ing, Is ev - er more with me.

Chorus

2 O Mary, mild-eyed Mary.
   By land or on the sea.
   Though time and tide may vary,
   My heart beats true to thee.

   Chorus

3 With thy fair face before me,
   How sweetly flew the hour,
   When all thy beauty o'er me
   Came streaming in its power.

   Chorus

4 The face with kindness glowing,
   The face that hides no guile,
   The light grace of thy going,
   The witchcraft of thy smile !

   Chorus

5 And when with blossoms laden
   Bright summer comes again,
   I'll fetch my nut-brown maiden
   Down from the bonny glen.

   Chorus

Bonnie George Campbell

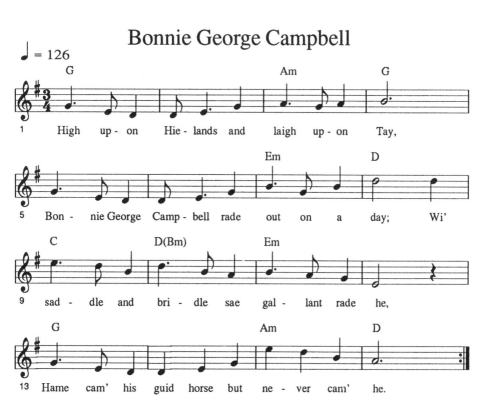

♩ = 126

1 High up - on Hie - lands and laigh up - on Tay,

5 Bon - nie George Camp - bell rade out on a day; Wi'

9 sad - dle and bri - dle sae gal - lant rade he,

13 Hame cam' his guid horse but ne - ver cam' he.

Doun cam' his mither dear, greetin' fu' sair;
And out cam' his bonnie wife rivin' her hair;
'My meadows lie green, and my corn is unshorn,
My barn is to bigg, and I'm left a' forlorn !'

'Saddled and booted and bridled rade he,
A plume in his helmet, a sword at his knee;
But toom cam' the saddle a' bluidy to see,
Oh, hame cam' his guid horse, but never cam' he !'

OMB 94

I'm a Rover and Seldom Sober

♩ = 84

1 *Chorus:* I'm a ro - ver and sel - dom so - ber, I'm a
4 ro - ver o' high deg - ree; It's when I'm drink - ing I'm al - ways
7 think - ing, How to gain my love's com - pa - ny.

Though the night be as dark as dungeon,
No' a star to be seen above,
I will be guided without a stumble
Into the airms o' my ain true love.

He steppit up to her bedroom window,
Kneelin' gently upon a stone,
He rappit at her bedroom window;
'Darlin' dear, do you lie alone?'

She raised her head on her snaw white pillow,
Wi' her airms aboot her breast,
'Wha' is that at my bedroom window,
Disturbing me at my lang night's rest?'

'It's only me, your ain true lover,
Open the door and let me in,
For I hae come on a lang journey
And I'm near drenched unto the skin.'

She opened the door wi' the greatest pleasure,
She opened the door and she let him in.
They baith shook hands and embraced each other,
Until the morning they lay as one.

The cocks were crawin', the birds were whistlin',
The burns they ran free abune the brae;
'Remember lass, I'm a ploughman laddie
And the fairmer I must obey.'

'Noo ma love, I must go and leave you,
Tae climb the hills, they are far above;
But I will climb them wi' the greatest pleasure,
Since I've been in the airms o' ma love.

OMB 94

O Lassie Art Ye Sleepin' Yet ?

♩ = 104

Thou hear'st the winter wind an' weet;
Nae star blinks thro' the driving sleet;
Tak pity on my weary feet,
    And shield me frae the rain, jo.

Chorus

The bitter blast that round me blaws,
Unheeded howls, unheeded fa's;
The cauldness o' thy heart's the cause
    Of a' my care and pine, jo.

Chorus

O tell na me o' wind an' rain,
Upbraid na me wi' cauld disdain,
Gae back the gate ye cam again,
    I winna let ye in, jo.

New Chorus:

I tell you now this ae night,
This ae, ae, ae night;
And ance for a' this ae night,
I winna let ye in, jo.

The snellest blast, at mirkest hours,
That round the pathless wand'rer pours
Is nocht to what poor she endures,
  That's trusted faithless man, jo.

New Chorus

The sweetest flower that deck'd the mead,
Now trodden like the vilest weed—
Let simple maid the lesson read
  The weird may be her ain, jo.

New Chorus

The bird that charm'd his summer day,
And now the cruel fowler's prey;
Let that to witless woman say
  The gratefu' heart of man, jo !

New Chorus

OMB 54

Hey Ca' Thro'

We hae tales to tell,
An' we hae sangs to sing;
We hae pennies to spend,
An' we hae pints to bring.

Chorus

We'll live a' our days,
And them that comes behin'
Let them do the like,
An' spend the gear they win.

Chorus

The Cruel Mither

♩ = 80

A mi - ni - ster's doch - ter in the north,

Hey, the rose and the lin - sie- o, She's fa'en in love with her

faith - er's clerk, Doon by the green - wood si - die - o.

2 She's coorted him a year and a day,
Hey the Rose etc.
Till her the young man did betray.
Doon by the etc.

3 She leaned her back against a tree,
And there the tear did blin' her e'e.

4 She leaned her back against a thorn,
And there twa bonnie boys has she born.

5 She's ta'en the napkin frae her neck,
And made to them a winding sheet.

6 She's ta'en oot her wee penknife,
And quickly twined them o' their life.

7 She's laid them 'neath a marble stane,
Thinking to gang a maiden hame.

8 She looked ower her faither's wa',
And she's seen twa bonnie boys at the ba'.

9 'O bonnie bairns, gin ye were mine,
I would dress ye in the silk sae fine'.

10 'O cruel mither, when we were thine,
We didna see ocht o' silk sae fine'.

11 'O bonnie bairns, come tell to me,
Whit kind o' a deith I'll hae to dee'.

12 'Seven year a fish in the flood,
Seven years a bird in the wood.

13 Seven years a tongue to the warning bell,
Seven years in the caves o' hell'.

14 'Welcome, welcome, fish in the flood,
Welcome, welcome, bird in the wood.

15 Welcome tongue to the warning bell,
But God keep me frae the caves o' hell'.

OMB 94

Will Ye Gang Love ?

I wish, I wish, I wish in vain
I wish I were a maid again
But a maid again I never will be
Till an apple grows on an orange tree.

Chorus

I wish, I wish my babe was born
I wish it sat on his daddy's knee
An' I mysel' were deid an' gone
An' the wavin' grass all o'er me growin'.

Chorus

As lang as my apron did bide doon
He followed me frae toon tae toon
But noo it's up above ma knee
My love gaes by but he kens na me.

Chorus

Mak' my grave baith lang and deep
Put a bunch of roses at my head and feet,
And in the middle put a turtle dove,
Let the people know I died of love.

I Hae a Wife o' My Ain

♩. = 108

1. I hae a wife o' my ain, I'll par- take wi' nae- bo- dy,
2. I am nae- bo- dy's lord, I'll be slave to nae- bo- dy,

I'll tak cuck- old frae nane, I'll gie cuck- old to nae- bo- dy.
I hae a guid braid sword, I'll tak dunts frae nae- bo- dy

I hae a pen- ny to spend, There thanks to nae- bo- dy
I'll be mer- ry and free, I'll be sad for nae- bo- dy, If

I hae nae- thing to lend, I'll bor- row frae nae- bo- dy.
nae- bo- dy cares for me, I'll care for nae- bo- dy.

Blythe, Blythe and Merry was She

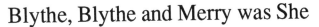

♩ = 116

Chorus

1. Blythe, blythe, and mer-ry was she. Blythe was she but and ben

5. Blythe by the banks o' Earn, And blythe in Glen-tur-rit glen. By

10. Ouch-ter-tyre there grows the aik, On Yar-row banks the bir-ken-shaw; But

14. Phe-mie was a bon-nier lass, Than braes o' Yar-row e-ver saw.

Chorus

Her looks were like a flow'r in May,
Her smile was like a simmer morn;
She tripped by the banks o' Earn,
As light's a bird upon a thorn.

Chorus

Her bonnie face it was as meek
As ony lamb upon a lea;
The evening sun was ne'er sae sweet,
As was the blink o' Phemie's e'e.

Chorus

The Highland hills I've wander'd wide,
And o'er the Lawlands I hae been;
But Phemie was the blythest lass
That ever trod the dewy green.

Chorus

OMB 94

The Keach in the Creel

♩ = 80

1 A fair young maid went up the street some fresh fish for to
5 buy, And a bon-nie clerk's fall'n in love wi' her And he's fol-lowed her by and
9 by, Rick-y doo-dum dae, doo-dum dae, Rick-y dick-y doo-dum dae.

2 'O where live ye, my bonnie lass,
  I pray thee tell to me;
  For gin the nicht were e'er sae mirk
  I wad come and visit thee.'
  Ricky doo etc.

3 'O my father he aye locks the door
  My mither keeps the key;
  And gin ye were ever sic a wily wight
  Ye canna win in to me.'
  Ricky doo etc.

4 But the clerk he had ae true brother,
  And a wily wight was he;
  And he has made a lang ladder,
  Was thirthy steps and three.
  Ricky doo etc.

5 He has made a cleek but and a creel,
  A creel but and a pin;
  And he's away to the chimley-top,
  And he's letten the bonnie clerk in.
  Ricky doo etc.

6 The auld wife, being not asleep.
  Heard something that was said;
  'I'll lay my life,' quo the silly auld wife,
  'There's a man in our dochter's bed.'
  Ricky doo etc.

7 The auld man he gat owre the bed,
  To see if the thing was true;
  But she's ta'en the bonny clerk in her arms,
  And covered him owre with blue.
  Ricky doo etc.

8 'O where are ye gaun now, father? she says,
  And where are ye gaun sae late ?
  Ye've disturbed me in my evening prayers,
  And O but they were sweet !'
  Ricky doo etc.

9 'O ill betide ye, silly auld wife,
  And an ill death may ye dee !
  She has the muckle buik in her arms,
  And she's praying for you and me.'
  Ricky doo etc.

10 The auld wife being not asleep
Then something mair was said;
'I'll lay my life,' quo the silly auld wife,
There's a man in our dochter's bed.'
Ricky doo etc.

11 The auld wife she got owre the bed
To see if the thing was true;
But what the wrack took the auld wife's fit ?
For into the creel she flew.
Ricky doo etc.

12 The man that was at the chimley-top,
Finding the creel was fu',
He wrappit the rape round his left shouther,
And fast to him he drew.
Ricky doo etc.

13 'O help! O help! O hinny now help!
O help, O hinny now!
For him that ye aye wished me to
He's carryin me off just now.'
Ricky doo etc.

14 'O if the foul thief's gotten ye,
I wish he may keep his haud;
For a' the lee lang winter nicht
Ye'll never lie in your bed.'
Ricky doo etc.

15 He's towed her up, he's towed her down,
He's towed her through an through;
O Gude assist ! quo the silly auld wife,
For I'm just departin' now.
Ricky doo etc.

16 He's towed her up, he's towed her down,
He's gien her a richt down-fa'
Till every rib in the auld wife's side
Play'd nick-nack on the wa.'
Ricky doo etc.

17 O the blue, the bonnie, bonnie blue,
And I wish the blue may do weel!
And every auld wife that's sae jealous o' her dochter,
May she get a good keach in the creel!
Ricky doo etc.

OMB 94

Blow the Candle Out

♩ = 112

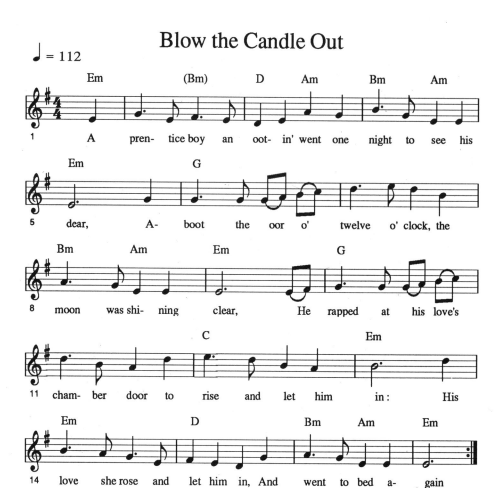

'Your father and your mother, love, do both in one bed lie
Embracing one another love, — how wouldn't you and I ?
The streets they are all crowded, with people going about;
I'll roll you in my arms, my dear, and blow the candle out.'

'And if you chance to have a son, you'll call him after me;
You'll nourish him and cherish him, and set him on your knee.
And when twelve months are over, my time it will be out,
And I'll come back and marry you, for blowin' the candle out.'

As true as I said and she had a son, she called him after me,
She nourished him and cherished him and set him on her knee,
And when twelve months were over, I thought my time was out,
But they've doubled my indenture for blowin' the candle out.'

Come all you that are prentice boys, a warning take by me;
If ever you go out at late your sweethearts for to see;
If you do as I have done, you need not be in doubt,
They'll double your indenture for blowing the candle out.

OMB 94

Will Ye No Come Back Again ?

♩ = 96

F   Bb   F

1 Bon - nie Char- lie's noo a - wa'; Safe - ly owre the

C   F   Bb   F

4 friend - ly main; Mo - ny a heart will break in twa,

C   F   Chorus:

7 Should he ne'er come back a - gain? Will ye no come

Dm   Bb   F   C

10 back a - gain? Will ye no come back a - gain?

F   Bb   F   C   F

13 Bet - ter lo'ed ye can - na be, Will ye no come back a - gain?

2 Ye trusted in your Hieland men,
They trusted you, dear Charlie !
They kent your hiding in the glen,
Death and exile braving.

Chorus

3 English bribes were a' in vain,
Tho' puir and puirer we maun be;
Siller canna buy the heart
That aye beats warm for thine and thee.

Chorus

4 We watch'd thee in the gloamin' hour,
We watch'd thee in the mornin' grey;
Tho' thirty thousand pounds they gie,
Oh, there is nane that wad betray !

Chorus

5 Sweet's the laverock's note, and land,
Liltin' wildly up the glen;
But aye to me he sings ae sang—
'Will ye no come back again?'
Will ye no come back again?

Chorus

Lassie Lie Near Me

♩ = 108

Lang hae we parted been, Lassie, my dearie;
Now we are met again, Lassie lie near me.

Chorus
Near me, near me, Lassie lie near me.
Lang hast thou lain thy lane, Lassie lie near me.

A' that I hae endured,
Lassie, my dearie,
Here in thy arms is cured,
Lassie lie near me.

Say that you'll aye be true,
Never deceive me;
And I'll love nane but you,
Lassie lie near me.

If in love's bower we meet,
Lassie my dearie,
My joys would be complete,
Lassie lie near me.

OMB 94

My Ain Folk

₃₀ home in dear auld Scot-land, wi' my ain folk

O' their absent ane they're telling
The auld folk by the fire;
And I mark the swift tears welling
As the ruddy flame leaps high'r.
How the mither wad caress me, were I but by her side:
Now she prays that Heav'n will bless me,
Tho' the stormy seas divide.
And it's oh ! but I'm longing for my ain folk,
Tho' they be but lowly, puir and plain folk;
I am far beyond the sea, but my heart will ever be
At home in dear auld Scotland, wi' my ain folk.

33

The Wark of the Weavers

17 was- na for the wark o' the wea- vers.

There's some folk independent o' ither tradesmen's wark
For women need nae barber an' dykers need nae clerk;
But there's no ane o' them but needs a coat an' a sark,
Na, they canna want the wark o' the weavers.

Chorus

There's smiths and there's wrights and there's mason chiels an a',
There's doctors an' there's meenisters an' them that live by law,
An' oor freens that bide oot ower the sea in Sooth America,
An' they a' need the wark o' the weavers.

Chorus

Oor sodgers an' oor sailors, od, we mak' them a' bauld
For gin they hadna claes, faith they couldna fecht for cauld;
The high an' low, the rich an' puir— a' body young an' auld,
They a' need the wark o' the weavers.

Chorus

So the weavin' is a trade that never can fail
Sae lang's we need ae cloot tae haud anither hale,
Sae let us a' be merry ower a bicker o' guid ale,
An' drink tae the health o' the weavers.

Chorus

OMB 94

John Anderson, My Jo

♩ = 116

John An- der- son my jo, John, When we were first ac-
quent, your locks were like the ra- ven, Your bon- nie brow was
brent; But now your brow is bald, John, your locks are like the
snaw, But bles- sings on your fros- ty pow, John An- der- son, my jo.

John Anderson, my jo, John,
We climb the hill together;
And mony a cantie day John,
We've had wi' ane anither:
Now we maun totter down, John,
And hand in hand we'll go,
And sleep thegither at the foot,
John Anderson, my jo.

Bonnie Annie

♩ = 108

There was a rich merchant wha cam' frae Dumbarton,
And he's got this bonnie lass big, big wi' bairn.

'Ye'll tak' ship wi' me and ye'll be my honey;
What more could a woman do than I'll do for ye ?'

'O captain, tak' gold, O captain, tak' money,
And steer for dry land for the sake of my honey.'

'How can I tak' gold, how can I tak' money ?
There's fey folk on my ship, she winna sail for me.'

'Tak' me by the fingers and lift me up heely,
And throw me owre board and hae nae pity on me.'

He's ta'en her by the fingers and did lift her up heely
And thrown her owre board though she was his ain dearie.

Her goon it was wide and her petticoat narrow,
And she swam afore them till they cam' to Yarrow.

His love she was there when they ca'd to dry land,
And her lyin' deid on the saut-sea strand.

Her baby was born and lyin' at her feet,
For the loss of his bonnie love sair did he greet.

He's caused mak' a kist o' the gowd sae yellow,
And they a' three sleep in the braes o' Yarrow.

OMB 94

Flow Gently Sweet Afton

♩ = 76

Flow gent- ly, sweet Af- ton! a- mong thy green braes, Flow gent- ly, I'll sing thee a song in thy praise; My Ma- ry's a- sleep by thy mur- mur- ing stream, Flow gent- ly, sweet Af- ton, dis- turb not her dream.

Thou stock dove whose echo resounds thro' the glen,
Ye wild whistling blackbirds in yon thorny den,
Thou green crested lapwing, thy screaming forbear,
I charge you, disturb not my slumbering Fair.

How lofty, sweet Afton, thy neighbouring hills,
Far mark'd with the courses of clear, winding rills;
There daily I wander as noon rises high,
My flocks and my Mary's sweet cot in my eye.

How pleasant thy banks and green valleys below,
Where, wild in the woodlands, the primroses blow;
There oft, as mild Ev'ning weeps over the lea,
The sweet-scented birk shades my Mary and me.

The crustal stream, Afton, how lovely it glides,
And winds by the cot where my Mary resides;
How wanton thy waters her snowy feet lave,
As, gathering sweets flowerets, she stems thy clear wave.

Flow gently, sweet Afton, amang thy green braes,
Flow gently, sweet river, the theme of my lays;
My Mary's asleep by thy murmuring stream,
Flow gently, sweet Afton, disturb not her dream.

OMB 94

Roy's Wife o' Aldivalloch

♩ = 104

As we cam' toddlin' roun' the Buck,
It's Roy gaed belgin' thro' the Balloch,
Weary fa' the faithless quean,
She's on the road to Aldivalloch.

Chorus

As we cam in about the Buck,
She cam' in about the Balloch,
Roy's piper play'd fu' weel
She's welcome hame to Aldivalloch.

Chorus

Tho' ye wad ca' the Cabrach wide
Frae Ordestan into the Balloch,
Ye wadna get sae swack a quean
As Roy's wife o' Aldivalloch.

Chorus

O, she is a canty quean,
And weel can dance Highland Walloch
Frae tap to tae sae tight and clean
It's Roy's wife o' Aldivalloch.

Chorus

Her hair sae fair, her e'en sae clear
Her wee bit mou' sae sweet and bonnie
To me she ever will be dear
Tho' she for ever left her Johnnie.

Chorus

But Roy's wife is scarce saxteen
Her days as yet hae nae been monie,
Roy's thrice as auld and turned again
She's taen the carle and left her Johnnie

Chorus

OMB 94

The Border Widow's Lament

♩ = 69

My love he built me a bon- nie bow'r, And clad it a' wi' li- lye- flow'r, A braw- er bow'r ye ne'er did see, Than my true love he built for me.

2 There came a man by middle day
   He spied his sport and went away
   And brought the king that very night
   Who brake my bow'r and slew my knight.

3 He slew my knight, to me sae dear
   He slew my knight, and pin'd his gear;
   The servants all for life did flee
   And left me in extremitie.

4 I sew'd a sheet, making my mane,
   I watch'd the corpse myself alane;
   I watch'd beside it night and day;
   Nae living creature came that way.

5 I took his body on my back
   And while I gaed, and while I sate;
   I digg'd a grave and laid him in
   And happ'd him with the sod sae green.

6 But think na ye my heart was sair,
   When I laid the mould on his yellow hair ?
   O, think na ye my heart was wae,
   When I turn'd about awa' to gae ?

7 Nae living man I'll love again,
   Since that my lovely knight is slain !
   Wi' ae lock o' his yellow hair,
   I'll chain my heart for evermair !

The Lothian Hairst

♩ = 76

On Au-gust the twelfth frae Ai-ber-deen, we sailed a-board the Prince, And land-ed safe on Staf-ford's field, with har-vest to com-mence

2 For six lang weeks the country roon
  Frae toon tae toon we went,
  We took richt weel wi' the Lothian chiels
  And were aye richt weel content.

3 Oor gaffer, Willie Mathieson
  Frae sweet Deeside he came
  Oor foreman cam' frae that same place
  And Logan was his name.

4 We followed Logan on the point
  And weel he laid it doon,
  And nimbly did he lead oor squad
  Owre mony the thristlie toon.

5 My mate and me we had nae chance
  For Logan's watchful eye;
  My mate and me we got nae slack
  For Logan was sae fly.

6 He cleared the bothy every nicht
  Before he went tae sleep,
  And not sae much as ane did leave
  But strict his rules did keep.

7 Fareweel MacKenzie, Reid and Rose
  And the rest o' the merry crew,
  There's Chalmers, Shepherd, Logan, Jock
  And the Royal Stewarts too.

8 It's I mysel', a Hielan' lad
  Wad wish nae better cheer
  Than a Lothian lass and a weel-made bed
  And a nicht as lang's a year.

9 Come fill oor glass and drink it doon
  Before oor boat shall start,
  And may we safely reach the shore
  And all in friendship part.

OMB 94

Dainty Davie

♩ = 108

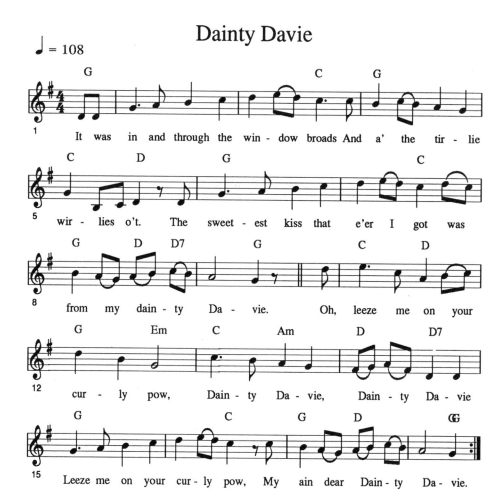

It was doon amang my daddy's pease,
And underneath the cherry trees—
Oh, there he kist me as he pleased,
For he was my ain dear Davie.

Chorus

When he was chased by a dragoon,
Into my bed he was laid doon,
I thocht him worthy o' his room,
For he's aye my dainty Davie.

Chorus

Will Ye Gang to Sherramuir ?

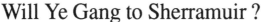

1 Will ye gang to Sher-ra-muir, Bauld John o' In-nis-ture,

3 There to see the no-ble Mar, And his Hie-land lad-dies?

5 A' the true men o' the north, An-gus, Hunt-ly and Sea-forth,

7 Scour-ing on to cross the Forth, Wi' their white cock-a-dies!

1 There you'll see the banners flare,
There you'll hear the bagpipes rair,
And the trumpets' deadly blair
Wi' the cannon's rattle.
There you'll see the bauld M'Craws,
Cameron's and Clandonald's raws,
And a' the clans wi' loud huzzas,
Rushing to the battle.

Chorus

2 There you'll see the noble Whigs
A' the heroes o' the brigs
Raw hides and wither'd wigs
Riding in array, man.
Riv'n hose and raggit hools,
Sour milk and girnin' gools,
Psalm-beuks and cutty-stools,
We'll see never mair, man.

Chorus

3 Will ye gang to Sherramuir
Bauld John o' Innisture?
Sic a day and sic an hour
Ne'er was in the north, man.
Siccan sights will there be seen;
And, gin some be nae mistaen,
Fragrant gales will come bedeen,
Frae the water o' Forth, man.

Chorus

OMB 94

A Scottish Soldier

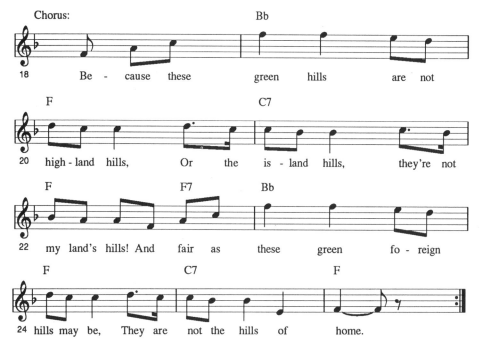

Chorus:

Be - cause these green hills are not high - land hills, Or the is - land hills, they're not my land's hills! And fair as these green fo - reign hills may be, They are not the hills of home.

And now this soldier, this Scottish soldier,
Who wander'd far away and soldiered far away,
Sees leaves are falling and death is calling,
And he will fade away, in that far land !
He called his piper, his trusty piper,
And bade him sound a lay, a pibroch sad to play,
Upon a hillside, a Scottish hillside,
Not on these green hills of Tyrol.

Chorus

And so this soldier, this Scottish Soldier,
Will wander far no more and soldier far no more,
And on a hillside, a Scottish Hillside,
You'll see a piper play, his 'Soldier Home'!
He'd seen the glory, he'd told his story,
Of battles glorious, and deeds victorious,
The bugles cease now, he is at peace now,
Far from those green hills of Tyrol.

Chorus

OMB 94

Fine Flowers in the Valley

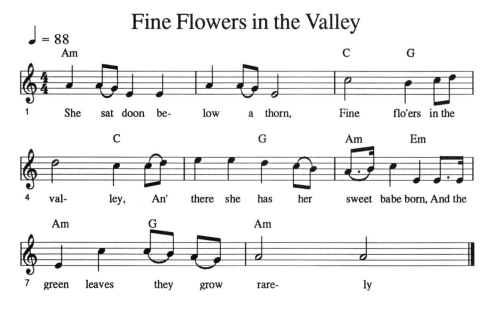

♩ = 88

1. She sat doon be-low a thorn, Fine flo'ers in the
4. val-ley, An' there she has her sweet babe born, And the
7. green leaves they grow rare-ly

'Smile na sae sweet, my bonnie babe,'
Fine flowers in the valley,
'An' ye smile sae sweet, ye'll smile me deid.'
And the green leaves they grow rarely.

She's ta'en oot her little pen-knife,
Fine flowers in the valley,
And twinn'd the sweet babe o' its life.
And the green leaves they grow rarely.

She's howket a grave by the light o' the moon,
Fine flowers in the valley,
And there she's buried her sweet babe in.
And the green leaves they grow rarely.

As she was going to the church,
Fine flowers in the valley,
She saw a sweet babe in the porch.
And the green leaves they grow rarely.

'O sweet babe, an' thou were mine,
Fine flowers in the valley,
I wad cleed thee in the silk fine.'
And the green leaves they grow rarely.

'O mither dear, when I was thine,
Fine flowers in the valley,
Ye didna prove tae me sae kind.'
And the green leaves they grow rarely.

The Men o' the North

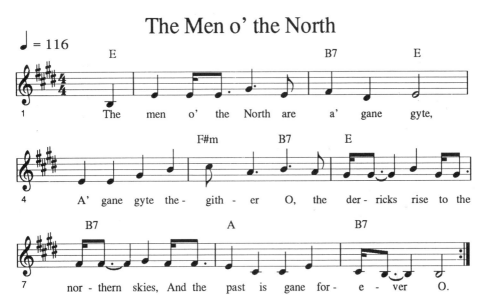

As I cam in by Peterheid
I saw it changin' sairly O,
For the tankers grey stand in the bay
And the oil is flowing rarely O.

Chorus

The lads frae the Broch hae left the fairm
Aff tae the rigs they're rushin' O,
For ye get mair pay for an oil-man's day
So they heed na the ploo nor the fishin' O.

Chorus

I met wi' a man frae Aiberdeen
That city aye sae bonnie O,
He said: 'There's a spree by the dark North Sea
And an affa smell o' money O.'

Chorus

What wad ye gie for the gowden sand
The whaup's cry in the morning O,
The rowan fair and the caller air
An the tide as it's gently turnin' O ?

Chorus

OMB 94

To Daunton Me

For a' his meal and a' his maut,
For a' his fresh beef and his saut,
For a' his gold and white monie,
An auld man shall never daunton me.

Chorus

His gear may buy him kye and yowes,
His gear may buy him glens and knowes;
But me he shall not buy nor fee,
For an auld man shall never daunton me

Chorus

He hirples twa-fold as he dow,
Wi' hi teethless gab and his auld beld pow,
And the rain rains down frae his red blear'd e'e;
That auld man shall never daunton me.

Chorus

A NOBLE MAIDEN SURVEYING A LANDSCAPE WHILE RESTRAINING
A RESTIVE HORSE.

OMB 94

Uist Tramping Song

17   wel- come that a- waits us,   Ere the   sun   goes   down.

It's the call of sea and shore
It's the tang of bog and peat,
And the scent of brier and myrtle
That puts magic in our feet;
So it's on we go rejoicing,
Over bracken, over stile,
And it's soon we will be tramping
Out the last long mile.

Chorus

OMB 94

The Twa Corbies

♩ = 96

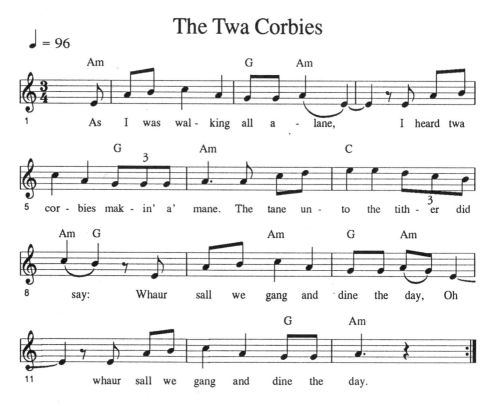

As I was wal-king all a-lane, I heard twa cor-bies mak-in' a' mane. The tane un-to the tith-er did say: Whaur sall we gang and dine the day, Oh whaur sall we gang and dine the day.

It's in ahint yon auld fail dyke
I wot there lies a new slain knight;
And naebody kens that he lies there
But his hawk and his hound, and his lady fair O
But his hawk and his hound, and his lady fair.

His hound is to the hunting gane
His hawk to fetch the wild-fowl hame,
His lady ta'en anither mate,
So we may mak' our dinner swate O,
So we may mak' our dinner swate.

Ye'll sit on his white hause-bane,
And I'll pike oot his bonny blue e'en
Wi' ae lock o' his gowden hair
We'll theek oor nest when it grows bare O
We'll theek oor nest when it grows bare.

There's mony a ane for him maks mane
But nane sall ken whaur he is gane
O'er his white banes when they are bare
The wind sall blaw for evermair, O
The wind sall blaw for evermair.

Donal' Don

♩ = 100

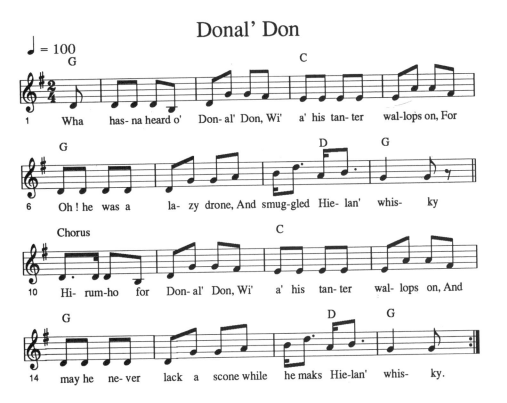

1 Wha has-na heard o' Don-al' Don, Wi' a' his tan-ter wal-lops on, For

6 Oh! he was a la-zy drone, And smug-gled Hie-lan' whis-ky

Chorus

10 Hi-rum-ho for Don-al' Don, Wi' a' his tan-ter wal-lops on, And

14 may he ne-ver lack a scone while he maks Hie-lan' whis-ky.

2 When first he cam' tae auld Dundee
'Twas in a smeeky hole lived he;
Where gauger bodies couldna see,
He played the king a pliskie.

Chorus

3 When he was young an' in his prime,
He lo'ed a bonny lassie fine;
She jilted him an' aye sin' syne
He's dismal, dull and dusky.

Chorus

4 A bunch o' rags is a' his braws,
His heathery wig wad fricht the craws;
His dusky face and clorty paws,
Wad fyle the bay o' Biscay.

Chorus

5 He has a sark, he has but ane,
It's fairly worn tae skin an' bane,
A-loupin', like tae rin its lane
Wi' troopers bauld and frisky.

Chorus

6 Whene'er his sark's laid out tae dry
It's Donald in his bed maun lie,
An' wait till a' the troopers die,
Ere he gangs oot wi' whisky.

Chorus

7 So here's a health tae Donal' Don,
Wi' a' his tanterwallops on,
An' may he never lack a scone
While he mak's Hieland whisky.

Chorus

OMB 94

The Gypsy Laddie

Lord Castles' lady came down the stair
And all her maidens behind her O
She had a bottle of the red wine in her hand
For to treat all the gypsy laddies wi' O

She's treated them a' wi' a bottle of red wine
Likewise with a little ginger O
Till one of them stepped up by her side
Stole the gold ring from off her finger O.

'It's you'll cast off your bonny silken dress
Put on my tartan plaidie O
And you' awa the lee lang day
For to follow the gypsy laddie O'.

She's casten off her bonny silken dress
Putten on his tartan plaidie
And she's awa' the lee lang day
For to follow the gypsy laddie O.

Lord Castles he came home at night
Inquiring for his lady
The one denied, and the other replied
She's awa' wi' the gypsy laddies O.

Make haste, make haste my milkwhite steed
Make haste and soon be ready
For I will neither eat no drink
Or I get back my lady O.

They've rode east and they've rode west
Until they cam to yonder boggy
And there the spied the pretty girl
Wi' the gipsies a' stanin' roon her O.

'It's you'll come back and back you'll come
It's you'll come back to me, my lady
For I will neither eat nor drink
Or ye come back aside me O'.

'I winna come back, my ain guid lord
Nor will I come back aside ye
For I've made a vow, and I will keep it true
For to follow the gypsy laddies O'.

Haven't ye gotten gold, love and haven't you gotten store
And haven't ye gotten treasures three
And haven't ye gotten all that ye want
And three bonny boys to amuse ye wi?'

Oh yes my lord I have gotten gold and store
Oh yes I have gotten treasures three
Oh yes I have gotten all that I want
And three bonny boys to amuse me wi'

There is sixteen o' you, a' great men
And none o' you to ca' bonny O
But ye shall all hanged be
For the stealin' awa' Lord Castles' lady O.

Last night I lay on a feather bed
And my great lord aside me O
But this night I lie on a caul' open van
And the gypsies a' lyin' roon me O.

OMB 94

Dance to your Daddie

♩ = 104

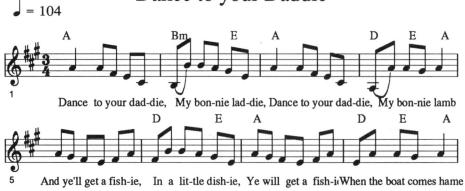

Dance to your dad-die, My bon-nie lad-die, Dance to your dad-die, My bon-nie lamb

And ye'll get a fish-ie, In a lit-tle dish-ie, Ye will get a fish-ie When the boat comes hame

Dance to your dad-die, My bon-nie lad-die, Dance to your dad-die, My bon-nie lamb !

Dance to your daddie, my bonnie laddie,
Dance to your daddie, my bonnie lamb !
And ye'll get a coatie, and a pair o' breekies,
Ye will get a whippie, and some bread and jam.

Repeat first verse

Bogie's Bonnie Belle

To work his twa best horses, cart or harrie, or ploo
Or onything aboot farmwork I very weel could do.

Aul' Bogie had a daughter, her name was Isabel
The lily of the valley and the primrose of the dell.

When she went a-walking, she chose me for her guide
Doon by the burn o' Cairnie to watch the fishes glide.

I threw my arms around her waist, frae her her feet did slide
And there she lay contented on Cairnie's burnie side.

The first three months were scarecely o'er, the lassie lost her bloom,
The red fell frae her bonny cheeks and her een began to swoon.

The next nine months were passed and gone, she brought me forth a son,
And I was quickly sent for, to see what could be done.

They said that I should marry her, but oh that would na dee
Said : 'You're nae match for my bonnie Belle and she's nae match for thee.'

But noo she's married a tinker lad, he comes frae Huntly toon,
He mends pots and pans and paraffin lamps, and he scours the country 'roon.

May be she's gotten a better match, aul' Bogie canna tell,
Fareweel ye lads o' Huntly side, and Bogie's bonnie Belle.

OMB 94

Lassie wi' the Yellow Coatie

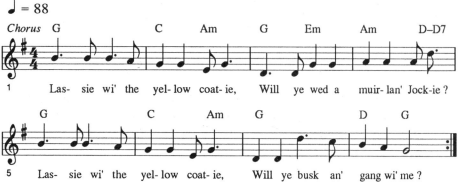

Although my mailen be but sma',
An' little gowd I hae to shaw,
I hae a heart without a flaw,
An' I will gie it a' to thee.

Chorus

Wi' my lassie an' my doggie,
O'er the lea an' through the boggie,
Nane on earth was e'er sae vogie,
Or as blythe as we will be.

Chorus

Haste ye lassie, to my bosom
While the roses are in blossom;
Time is precious, dinna lose them —
Flowers will fade, an' sae will ye.

Final Chorus :
Lassie wi' the yellow coatie,
Ah ! tak' pity on your Jockie;
Lassie wi' the yellow coatie,
I'm in haste, an' sae should ye.

A Brief Guide to the Songs

Although in no way meant to be comprehensive, the following notes will give as far as is relevant and traceable some idea of the background of each song in this volume.

5. I AINCE LO'ED A LASS

This song seems related to two other 'false bride' type songs, namely: 'Green grows the Laurel', and an old song, popular in Ireland: 'The Lambs on the Green Hills'.

aince — once; a' ithers — all others; flooers — flowers

6. THE ROAD TO THE ISLES

From volume II of 'Songs of the Hebrides,' collected and arranged by Marjory Kennedy-Fraser (1857-1930) and Kenneth Macleod. The three volumes of songs and tunes collected in the Hebrides around the turn of the century are testimony to an incredible richness of music on the islands as well as an indefatigable spirit of musical adventure on the part of the writers. With hindsight of course, it is easy to point out that the arrangements (for piano and harp) took away a lot of the free-flowing original Gaelic versions as sung by the countless ordinary islanders who sang for them. The original air of this song was played on the pipe-chanter by Malcolm Johnson of Barra. In its present form it was arranged by Patuffa Kennedy-Fraser, with rather doggerellish words by Kenneth MacLeod.

cromak — a crook-handled walking stick

8. SCOTLAND THE BRAVE

A well-known and spirited march tune, probably from the last century, with words by Cliff Hanley (a lowly poetic endeavour, really) and first published in this form in the 1950s by Kerr's of Glasgow.

10. HEY THE DUSTY MILLER

From Johnson's 'Museum'. The first two stanzas are Burns's contribution to this old song.

leeze me — I'm very pleased; siller — silver; wad — would; gie — give

11. GREEN GROW THE RASHES O

Words by Robert Burns. The tune of this song has a long pedigree, going back as far as the lute book manuscript of Sir Robert Gordon of Straloch (1627), where it is found as 'Green Greus ye Rasses. A Daunce'. Both the tune and Burns's lyrics

OMB 94

are exquisite. Once more, Burns took an old favourite ditty, regarded by decent folk as having 'indelicate' words, and re-wrote the song with superb insight into what was poetically memorable and musically natural. 'Green Grow' and 'A Man's a Man for All That' are two songs deserving to be as well-known as 'Auld Lang Syne' for their international and timeless sentiments.

rashes — rushes; cannie/canny — quiet(ly); e'en — evening; tapsalteerie — topsy-turvy; sae douce — so kind/pleasant

12. JOHNNIE COPE
With so many songs lamenting assorted massacres, defeats and fleeing kings, it was to be expected that an event such as the multiple victory of Highlandmen over badly-led Royalist troops under John Cope, would be exploited in a song such as this. The song celebrates the battle of Prestonpans (Sept 21, 1745) where Cope got his reputation for being the ultimate coward: he had fled in great haste and was the first to arrive safely at Berwick. It was said that 'he was the first general in Europe, who had brought the first tidings of his own defeat.' The words are by Adam Skirving (1719-1803), a farmer from Haddingtonshire in Lothian.

an ye daur — if you dare; waukin — wakened; frichtet — frightened; rin — run; hale — whole; spiered at — asked/inquired of

14. HORO MY NUT-BROWN MAIDEN
This is a translation of an old Gaelic song 'Ho ro mo nighean dhonn bholdheach', from the hand of professor John Stuart Blackie (1809-1895). Blackie, who, apart from being the prime Greek scholar of the day, had a tremendous interest in things Scottish and often fought an uphill battle to convince his peers of the genuineness of the songs and poetry of the 'plain people'. When Blackie found Scottish people attacking their own musical heritage by calling it 'vulgar,' he retorted with: 'Is it vulgar to be true to nature, to hate all affection, and call a spade a spade roundly, as Shakespeare did, and the English Bible, and Robert Burns? Is it vulgar to be patriotic, and love the land from which came to you from your father's blood and with your mother's milk? Is it vulgar to pour forth from the heart melody of native growth as fresh and bright and strong as the heather on the Scottish braes, . . . instead of piping forth soap-bells of shallow sentiment to tickle the ear of dreamy girls and shallow fopling in a drawing-room?'

15. BONNIE GEORGE CAMPBELL

(Child 210) This song only appears in a handful of printed collections and yet has maintained its popularity since it was written c.1800. 'It is supposed to be a lament for one of the adherents of the house of Argyle, who was killed in the battle of Glenlivat, 3rd October, 1594.' (Alfred Moffat in 'The Minstrelsy of Scotland' 1896).

laigh — low; greetin — weeping; fu' sair — pitifully (litt. full sore); rivin' — tearing; toom — empty; bluidy — bloody

16. I'M A ROVER AND SELDOM SOBER

Although it seems related to other well established old songs, it is hard to be definite about either the words or tune of this very popular song. The version given here is very much the way most people sing it nowadays.

18. O LASSIE ART YE SLEEPIN' YET?

Also known as 'O Let Me in This Ae Nicht.' This song was fashioned by Robert Burns out of an existing and allegedly 'more witty than decorous' song, at the behest of his publisher Johnson. While he was at it, Burns even provided the song with 'The Answer' - (the part after verse four). The air is ancient and even appeared in a virginal book where it is called 'The Newe Gowne Made.'

waukin' I wad wit — waking I'd like to know; fit — foot; fain be — love to be; jo — dear (joy); ae.. — (here) this very night (emphatic); weet — wet/rain; na/nae — no; winna — will not; snellest — hardest/most severe; weird — fate; ain — own

20. HEY CA' THRO'

Words by Robert Burns. It has been suggested that this song is an adaptation of an earlier piece or else new words set to the tune 'Carls O' Dysart'. The places mentioned in the first verse are fishing villages on the coast of Fife, where Burns visited and may indeed have collected the original song in one of these localities in 1787. Prior to this it had never appeared in print.

carls — old men; kimmers — old women; ca' thro' — lit. call through (work with a will); mickle/muckle/meikle ado — much to do; gear — wealth/possessions

21. THE CRUEL MITHER

From the Child Collection (Nr 20). The morbid theme of infanticide was

OMB 94

common enough in European folklore. Although this fine ballad contains some lovely poetic imagery, it must have been originally conceived as a moralizing tale. The first printed versions appeared in the last quarter of the 18th century. 'Linsie' - as in the refrain, is also spelled as Lindsay, or Lindsy. Our version is as sung by Ewan MacColl, who probably learned it from singers such as Jimmy McBeth or Jeannie Robertson. A quite unsettling 'comic' version of this song may be heard in Ireland where Dublin children will sing of 'she stuck the penknife in the baby's back, weila, weila, waile' - and all this accompanied by a merry little tune.

twined — parted; wa' — wall; ba' — ball; ocht — aught/anything; deith — death

22. WILL YE GANG, LOVE?

Known in many corners of the English-speaking world in a variety of versions. It also has some 'relations' in songs such as 'Careless Love' and 'Waly Waly.' The extraordinarily fine melody and words are best done justice by singing without any accompaniment, I feel.

chaumber — chamber; yellow — fair/blonde; gang — go; bide doon — stayed down; kens na — doesn't know

24. I HAE A WIFE OF MY AIN

Words by Robert Burns. A proud, successful and happy Burns has just married his 'Bonnie Jean' in 1788 and here extols the joy of living for all who care to hear. Set to an old dance tune of the same title.

hae — have; ain — own; frae nane — from none ; gude braid — good broad; dunts — blows/knocks

25. BLYTHE, BLYTHE AND MERRY WAS SHE

Words by Robert Burns. Based on the old song of 'Andro and his Cutty Gun'. Written in 1787, when Burns interrupted his Highland tour to stay at Ochtertyre house at Strathearn, where he met Euphemia Murray, a young cousin of his host.

but(t) and ben — kitchen and parlour; aik — oak; birken shaw — beech wood; ony — any; e'e — eye

26. THE KEACH IN THE CREEL

From Child's Collection (Nr 281). The prototype of this story may have originated in France where it was known as 'Du Chevalier a la Corbeille' at the end of the 14th century. This ballad appears in many forms - some featuring two repeating lines at the end of each stanza:

'And he's followed her by and by, by,
  And he's followed her by.'

In Motherwell's 'Minstrelsy' (Glasgow 1827) a charming version is printed under the title 'Ricadoo' which instead of the previous echoing last lines gives us:

'Ricadoo, tunaway, ricadoo a doo a day,
  Raddie ricadoo tunaway.'

Our version printed here makes use of yet a different source as well: Whitelaw's 'Book of Scottish Ballads' - where it is given as: 'taken down from the recitation of a gentleman in Liddesdale.'

mirk— dark; sic a wily wight — such a strong/clever person; canna win in — cannot come in; cleek — hook; creel — basket; muckle buik — the Bible; wrack — ruin/misfortune; fit — foot; rape — rope; lee lang — live-long; Gude assist — God help; gien — gave; down fa' — down fall/dropped; keach — pitch/toss aside/shake; The keach in the creel — The 'shaker' in the basket

28. BLOW THE CANDLE OUT
Collected in 1908 by Gavin Greig. Versions of this song with slight variations in both the words and/or music are found in Ireland and England as well.

30. WILL YE NO COME BACK AGAIN ?
Words by Lady Nairne, the air may be by Neil Gow Junior, grandson of the famous Neil. Yet another song celebrating, or perhaps lamenting, the eternal fugitive, Charles Edward Stuart (1720-1788). Bonnie Charlie, who in reality may not have quite deserved the unflinching loyalty of his Highland supporters, soon became a near-mythological hero. Countless poems and songs are dedicated to his continuous successes in hiding and fleeing, after the defeat at Culloden in 1746. Apart from the excellent songs thus created, his followers must have at least gotten some sense of consolation, pride and even glee out of them.

laverock — the lark; noo awa' — now away; puir — poor; siller — silver; aye — always; nane — none; wad — would

31. LASSIE LIE NEAR ME
A gorgeous love song, the 'bones' of which were found in the 'Scottish Musical Museum'. This present version features additional verses written by Peter Hall.

OMB 94

32. MY AIN FOLK

Although this song is immensely popular I've drawn a blank on its history and author. It certainly does not seem to be very ancient - the words are of a Victorian tear-jerking quality, while the music seems to have little to do with Scotland. In fact, the more I hear it, the more it sounds like something from a German light opera.

ain — own; shieling/sheiling — hut/shed/cottage; burn — stream/rivulet; puir — poor

34. THE WARK O' THE WEAVERS

From Ford's 'Vagabond Songs'. Ord in his 'Bothy Songs' makes the following observations: 'towards the middle of the last century, this spirited song was very popular in Forfarshire and other centres of the handloom weaving industry. Its author was a Forfar weaver, David Shaw, who published two small collections of his poems, the best of which are 'The Forfar Pensioner' and 'Tammie Treddlefeet'. He died in Forfar in 1856, in his seventieth year.'

a gither — together; tae crack — to have fun; wark — work; claith — cloth; wadna hae — wouldn't have; gin — if; od — mild oath: God!; oot o' oor woo' — out of our wool; no ane — not one; sark — shirt; canna want — here: couldn't do without; chiels — fellows/young men; oor freens — our friends; bauld — strong/fierce; hadna claes — had no clothes; fecht for cauld — fight because of the cold; puir — poor; ae cloot — a patch; tae haud anither hale — to patch another hole; bicker — drinking vessel (litt. beaker); a — all

36. JOHN ANDERSON, MY JO

Words by Robert Burns. Again, this is an old Scottish song, re-worked by Burns. Apart from some alterations, the first and last verses are entirely from Burns's goose quill. A tender and reflective piece that certainly has stood the test of time. It was first committed to paper in the 16th century.

my jo — my darling (joy); brent — smooth; beld pow — bald head; ane anither — one another

37. BONNIE ANNIE

This is known as a 'Jonah' ballad - an allusion to the main character in the story who has committed some form of crime and then wants to sail the salty seas into oblivion. Many versions of this ballad report the notion of the sailors drawing lots on who is to be thrown overboard - as an evil presence is perceived to endanger all their lives. The lot falls on poor Annie, (or did the brave sailors single out the only female on board?) who in her guilt- and grief-stricken mood asks the captain to lift her gently overboard. Apart from the quite unusual theme of the ballad, the tune too may be considered pretty unique - it consists out of just two of the briefest, succinct musical phrases imaginable. Perhaps because of the rise and fall of the music in each stanza it creates a slightly hypnotic effect.

fey — doomed; heely — carefully/gently; afore — before; sair did he greet — sorely he wept; kist — coffin/box; gowd — gold

38. FLOW GENTLY, SWEET AFTON
Words by Robert Burns. This song, together with only a few others, breathes very little of the earthy Scottishness of the main body of Burns' output. The rather genteel language may be something to do with the fact that he was nearly embarrassed with gratefulness towards a Mrs. Stewart of Afton, in Ayrshire, who was the first person of high station to recognize his genius. The song (1786) was dedicated to Mrs. Stewart, but the 'Slumbering Fair' of the song is likely to have been his own beloved 'Highland Mary', whom he courted in that year. Generally, this song has a lot in common with the type of songs Thomas Moore (who was roughly a contemporary) fashioned out of old Irish airs.

braes — slopes of hills; birk — beech tree

40. ROY'S WIFE OF ALDIVALLOCH
The tune is an old Highland air, previously published in Bremner's and Aird's collections under the title 'The Ruffian's Rant'. Burns set his song 'Canst thou leave me thus, my Katy' to the same air. The words were collected for the Greig-Duncan collection. A reduced set of words with a slightly different tune was claimed by Mrs. Grant of Carron (1745-1814) and appeared in many Scottish songbooks. John Roy, son of Thomas Roy of Aldivalloch was married to Isabella, daughter of Allister Stewart of Cabrach in February 1727. Isabel(la) took off with a younger man and as the song relates, an attempt was made by old Roy and his posse to retrieve the young girl.

Belgin' — bounding; quean — good-looking woman; swack — lithe/supple; tap to tae — top to toe; mou' — mouth; monie — many; carle — fellow/chap

42. THE BORDER LAMENT
An old ballad this, with only a handful of printed sources. It's likely to be an 18th cent. ballad and R.A. Smith, writing in 1824 reports that 'This lament is for

OMB 94

Cockburn of Henderland, whose grave is still visible, with many other memorials of lawless times.'

brawer — better/nicer; happ'd — covered (heaped); sair — sore; wae — tormented; ae — one

43. THE LOTHIAN HAIRST
A traditional Bothy ballad following the usual pattern of a fairly cheery tune coupled with a rich set of lyrics describing the toils, locations, personalities and often enough the humorous side of this glorified form of slave labour.

44. DAINTY DAVIE
From Herd's collection of 1776. It may of course be entirely fictitious but it has been alleged that the central character of this song was a Rev. David Williamson. The worthy Reverend had to flee some dragoons and took refuge in the house of Lady Cherrytree (with a name like that, you know it's a true story). She was so kind as to suggest to the poor fugitive that he might conceal himself in her daughters bed. Probably out of fear the poor man clung to the lass and ends up marrying her. In the 'Merry Muses of Caledonia' - a collection of smutty ditties written and collected by Robert Burns, there is a frank version of this lovely song:

> 'My minnie laid him at my back
> I trow he lay na lang at that
> But turn'd, and in a verra crack
> Produc'd a dainty davie.'

window broads — shutters; tirlie-wirlies — whirlygigs; leeze — blessing on; pow — head

45. WILL YE GANG TO SHERRAMUIR ?
From Hogg's 'Jacobite Relics of Scotland' of 1819. It was contributed by Hogg's correspondent Mr John Graham. The words are anonymous, possibly by the poet Tannahill. The battle of Sheriffmuir was fought in 1715, between the Duke of Argyle on the Royalist side and the Earl of Mar leading the rebels.

rair — roar; riv'n hose — ripped/torn pants; raggit hools — ragged covers (perh. cloaks); girnin' gools — twisted mouths; beuk — book; cutty stool — small three-legged stool of repentance, where sinners were made to sit and exposed publicly in church; bedeen — quickly

46. A SCOTTISH SOLDIER (*The Green Hills of Tyrol*)

This was a knock-out hit in the early '60's when Andy Stewart's recording of it rang right across the world. I seem to remember another vaudeville piece in similar style: 'Old Soldiers never die,' which around the same time was just as popular. The sentiments are a bit on the top-heavy side, but it's a great, grippin' auld song anyway!

pibroch — classical and ancient Scottish bagpipe music

48. FINE FLOWERS IN THE VALLEY

The air is reminiscent of 'Geordie', the words a variant of 'The Cruel mother'.

twinn'd - severed; howket - dug

49. THE MEN O' THE NORTH

This song was written by Sheila Douglas and appears in her excellent collection of songs : 'Sing a Song of Scotland'. She describes the many changes that have come over modern Scotland and finishes with a finely versed appeal to limit the despoilation of the country.

gane gyt — gone mad; aff tae — off to; ploo — plough; affa — awful; gowden — golden; whaup — the curlew; rowan — mountain ash; caller — fresh/cool/clear

50. TO DAUNTON ME

Words by Robert Burns. The air of this song is found in Oswald's 'Caledonian Pocket Companion' of c.1755 and also in McGibbon's 'Collection of Scots Tunes' edited by Bremner in 1762. A small volume of Jacobite songs entitled 'A Collection of Loyal Songs, Poems & c.' printed in 1750 contains a song known as 'The Song of the Chevalier', beginning with the line 'To daunton me'. It is possible that the tune may have been rewritten by McGibbon, who was 'a good composer and an excellent performer on the violin and an industrious collector and editor of Scots music'. The tune is also known as 'Lady Keith's Lament'. The song: 'When the King Comes Owre Water', which dates back to c.1745, was also written to the same tune.

blude-red — blood-red; blaw — bloom; daunton — conquer/control/subdue; maut — malt; saut — salt; kye and yowes — kine and ewes; glens and knowes — valleys and hills; hirples — limps/hobbles/drags; dow — can; beld pow — bald pate; blear'd e'e — bleary eye

OMB 94

52. UIST TRAMPING SONG
From: 'Songs of the Isles', by Hugh S. Roberton. Originally collected from Archibald MacDonald of Uist. English words by Roberton, tune (arranged) by J.R. Bannerman.

54. THE TWA CORBIES
I feel this is one of the most morbid and yet startlingly beautiful Scottish ballad-poems ever written. Also known as the 'Three Ravens' it was first printed in Ritson's 'Ancient Songs' of 1790. The words are nearly overpowering in their rude sense of showing our mortality. The original air has been in disuse for a while and it is nowadays sung to - of all things - a Breton tune. This Gaelic interchange came about as a result of a meeting between a Scots and a Breton musician in the 1960s. It was found that the ancient air of 'An Alarc'h' (the Swan) fitted absolutely perfectly.

twa — two; corbies — crows/ravens (from the French 'corbeau'); mane — moan/croak; tane — one; tither — other; whaur — where; ahint — behind; fail — turf; wot — know; swate — sweet; hause bone — collar bone; pike — pick; theek — thatch; maks mane — will mourn; sall ken — shall know

55. DONAL' DON
From Robert Ford's 'Vagabond Songs' (Paisley, 1899-1901). Donal's adventures while running his precarious off-licence make a great song and it must have been a favourite party piece for many years. It's hard to better some of the Scottish expressions such as 'tanterwallops' (rags).

drone — ass (from Gaelic for backside— dronn); smeeky — smoky; gauger bodies — excisemen; aye sin' syne — ever since then; braws — worldly goods; wad fright — would frighten; craws — crows; clorty — filthy; wad fyle — would foul; sark — shirt; skin an' bane — skin and bone; a-loupin' — dashing/running; tae rin its lane — to run alone/to be pursued

56. THE GYPSY LADDIE
This is one of a whole body of songs such as 'The Beggerman', 'The Jolly Beggar', 'The Pedlar' and others. The central theme is that of a swarthy stranger crossing the doorstep eventually resulting in elopements, abductions and/or dalliance of some kind or other. This song was also recorded in Ireland and is as well known there. The song features in many collections including Child (Nr 200). The events described may be largely fictitious, however, a gypsy by the name of Johnny Faa was executed in 1134 and all his folk were banished. Faa

appears as the culprit in some of the songs' versions as the roguish gypsy who carries off the wife of the Earl of Cassillis.

58. DANCE TO YOUR DADDIE
This dandling song is equally well-known in Northumbria. It has a lovely pulsating rhythm to it which shouldn't be overdone - a moderate tempo is essential!

59. BOGIE'S BONNIE BELLE
I've heard many versions of this old ballad and am always surprised that no matter how the words and tune are approached it somehow always sounds right. To me this is nothing less than a very special occurrence in both folk and classical music: sometimes a composition is simply so right, so powerful and yet so plain, that it just cannot be killed off. Bach's music, even when played on a kazoo or sung by a barbershop quartet still sounds right. Bogie's Bonnie Belle was recorded by Davie Stewart of Dundee and Jimmy McBeth of Elgin, amongst others. The feeing market referred to was an annual event where farmworkers signed up for a year's service with the landlords or farmers.

harrie — harrow; ploo — plough; would na dee — would not do; 'roon — around

60. LASSIE WI' THE YELLOW COATIE
Here's a song with a lot of scope for a good singer with a sense of musical phrasing; the rhythm need not be constrained by its common time framework. Many notes may be held on longer for effect. Written by James Duff (from: Poems and Songs, 1816). Another version is by John Hamilton (Song Gems, 1908).

coatie — frock/skirt; muirlan' — moorland; busk — get ready; kail — cabbage; a but an' ben — small, two-roomed cottage ; fu' genty — neat and tidy; mailen — farm; gowd — gold; shaw — show; sae vogie — so jaunty

OMB 94